CONVERSATIONS
DURING SLEEP

CONVERSATIONS DURING SLEEP

POEMS BY
MICHELE WOLF

1997 Anhinga Prize for Poetry
Selected by Peter Meinke

ANHINGA PRESS, 1998
TALLAHASSEE, FLORIDA

*This publication is sponsored in part by a grant from the Florida Department
of State, Division of Cultural Affairs, and the Florida Arts Council.*

Cover art: Rousseau, Henri. "The Sleeping Gypsy." 1897.
Oil on canvas, 51" x 6' 7" (129.5 x 200.7 cm).
The Museum of Modern Art, New York.
Gift of Mrs. Simon Guggenheim. Photograph © 1998
The Museum of Modern Art, New York.

Cover design, book design and production by Lynne Knight

Library of Congress Cataloging-in-Publication Data

Conversations During Sleep, Poems by Michele Wolf —
First Edition

ISBN 0938078-55-0 (cloth)
ISBN 0938078-56-9 (paper)
Library of Congress Cataloging Card Number 98-070429

Anhinga Press Inc. is a nonprofit corporation dedicated wholly
to the publication and appreciation of fine poetry.

For personal orders, catalogs and information
write to Anhinga Press,
P.O. Box 10595,
Tallahassee, FL 32302;
www.anhinga.org

Printed in the United States of America
First Edition, 1998

ACKNOWLEDGMENTS

My thanks to the editors of the following publications, where many of the poems in this collection first appeared:

The Antioch Review: "Flamingo Sunset"

Beyond Lament: Poets of the World Bearing Witness to the Holocaust, edited by Marguerite M. Striar, Northwestern University Press. Copyright © 1998: "Badge"

Boulevard: "The Keeper of Light"

Confrontation: "Fisherman," "Silent Night"

Connecticut River Review: "Inheritance"

Cottonwood Review: "When the Last Child Left"

Croton Review: "Typing in the Nude"

The Devil's Millhopper: "Solved in Sleep"

The Gallatin Review: "June 1978: Silver Anniversary"

Global City Review: "A Poet's Museum"

Hubbub: "Night Vision"

I Am Becoming the Woman I've Wanted, edited by Sandra Martz, Papier-Mâché Press. Copyright © 1994: "Response to a Reading"

Journal of Progressive Human Services: "The Spelling Champion," "Veterans Memorial"

The Ledge: "Artificial Breathing"

Matrix Women's Newsmagazine: "Badge"

The Ohio Poetry Review: "The Kinesthetic Observer"

Out of Season: An Anthology of Work By and About Young People Who Died, edited by Paula Trachtman, Amagansett Press. Copyright © 1993: "A Sister Far Away"

Painted Bride Quarterly: "Astigmatism," "Levitation"

Pequod: "Lucky Smile"

Pivot: "Miramar"

Poet Lore: "Healing Dirt"

Poetry: "Man With Picture Frame," "The Sleeping Gypsy"

Riverstone: "The Sacrifice and the Prayer"

Southern Poetry Review: "Astigmatism," "The Blind Spot"

When I Am an Old Woman I Shall Wear Purple, edited by Sandra Martz, Papier-Mâché Press. Copyright © 1987: "For My Mother"

The poems "The Diorama," "Keep Going," "Seizure," and "Toilette" were first published in *The Hudson Review.*

The following poems appeared in *The Keeper of Light (Painted Bride Quarterly* Poetry Chapbook Series. Copyright © 1995): "Astigmatism," "Flamingo Sunset," "Levitation," "June 1978: Silver Anniversary," "Response to a Reading," "The Diorama," "Conversations During Sleep," "Man With Picture Frame," "Toilette," "Lucky Smile," "The Spelling Champion," "For My Mother," "Inheritance," "Healing Dirt," "Badge," "Night Vision," "Solved in Sleep," "The Keeper of Light."

"Trees" received the 1997 Anna Davidson Rosenberg Award for Poems on the Jewish Experience special fiftieth-anniversary award for a poem related to Israel, sponsored by the Judah L. Magnes Museum in Berkeley, California.

I would like to thank the Bread Loaf Writers' Conference, the Corporation of Yaddo, the Edward F. Albee Foundation, the Helene Wurlitzer Foundation of New Mexico, and the Virginia Center for the Creative Arts for their support.

For Cathy Sharon Wolf,
in loving memory

CONTENTS

THREE

FOUR

CONVERSATIONS
DURING SLEEP

ONE

"THE SLEEPING GYPSY"

Henri Rousseau, 1897

In the heat of her dream, she hears
The iron kettle boiling, its scuttle and hum
As hurried as hoofbeats across a plain.
She drops in two guinea hens. Dancing
In a ring round her skirts, the children
Cheer, "Auntie, the English song!" Lifting
Her lute, she sings of the cat and the fiddle,
The cow jumping over the moon. How the little
Ones hoot when the dish runs away
With the spoon. Ah, spoon—an uncloaked
Lute, it waits to be strummed. The temptation
Of spoon. The temptation of London, of Paris,
Of bumping along in the carriage with M. Philippe
In his top hat and greatcoat to visit
The peacocks, turquoise and gold and green, each
Roaming the Bois de Boulogne with one hundred eyes.

She sleeps in the desert, under a smiling full moon
That shines in the teal night. Quiet behind her,
A lion stands, tail erect, having sniffed
At her onyx flesh, at the ribbony stripes
His color blindness darkens on her muslin dress,
All rainbow hues. She is lost in a dream,
Always happiest out of doors, without shoes.

KEEP GOING

I was led to the trees, as if someone with muscle
In her walk had pushed me. Heading
To the leaves—regal, molten with their final
Chance to breathe, Indian summer—I stopped
By the crowd shouting at the blue police barricade,
Mile 25. This was the moment, one of 26,000
Runners, you presented yourself, dazed and red-faced,
Soldiering on. Although I was too astonished
To speak, your name issued from me, the same way
A cut bleeds, the eyes allow us to see.
"Keep going!" I shouted, again without forethought.
Slowly, your mouth fashioned my name, then
You continued, working to control your body,
Pushing on through a life out of control.

"I can't sit still" were your words, so urgent,
Serving as much as a plea and apology as a goodbye.
Yet it is the way we would sit together
For which I remember you. We would talk only briefly
Or not talk, leaning against each other while the light
Turned to darkness over the Hudson, until we were sitting
In darkness, and one of us, without any active thought,
Might quietly speak, or rise to turn on a light,
Or move closer to the other, as if the darkness
Itself had spoken and thought were held away
Like an outsider, standing outside a barrier,
And we were not going anywhere. We were inside.

ASTIGMATISM

When I held smooth the satin to zip
Up your wedding dress, frosted with flounces
And pearl-beaded filigree, a rococo
Confection more sugary than the cake,
And watched as you swiveled slowly to face
Me — all floaty notes, pure flute — so still
As I situated the baby's breath and the veil,
How could I have told you, knowing
You'd learn it soon enough, my perfect doll,
How fuzzy the world is, how the clearest
Picture, frill-tipped gladioli in primary
Colors, can dissolve into darkness, how
The eye can fool you, presenting a straight
Or diagonal path when the earth is curved.

"It can be corrected," I tell you, a half-truth,
When you call me to say you can no longer
Focus, nothing is sharp. And I can hear
How the light is bent in your voice, the shadows
Behind what you say, while in my mind's
Eye you stare at me, blinking, a week old,
The day you were placed in my arms,
Able to distinguish little but two black
Moons, my eyes dancing in the fog.
That this was the most exquisite
Instance of my childhood never changes.
Nor does the decade between us
Or the way you looked up at my face
After racing out the front door
To greet me eight years later, almost
Toppling me over, ringing my waist.
Two sisters, so nearsighted

That upon my return to you, before
I resumed my groping tromp
Through the world, you held me like a reference
Point, a place you will always find,
The sheen of your eyes announcing
My bearings as much as your clear
Shout of my name, as your words: *"You're here."*

FLAMINGO SUNSET

While the bus horn bellowed, I knocked,
Swinging my swim bag, a dinghy maneuvering
Rough seas, received no answer.
Stepping into the room, I discovered a horror
Movie—*The Mom Who Turned Into a Dog.*
My hunched-over mother, her independent
Breasts as free-floating as limbs, clung
Drenched to my stepfather, beneath her,
Opaque in the shadows, grunting.
Locked stiff, I backed out, clicking
The door tight behind me, never to knock again.

Age almost twelve, I boarded the bus bound
For day camp, advancing, with my body
Narrowed, breast buds filling an A cup,
Into Flamingos, the oldest girls. A blue-ribbon
Artist, I spent weeks preparing pastel portraits
Of flamingos, plump and ruddy, their lush
Pink a stain on the memory, a cellophane
Wrapping masking the sky at dusk
While a flaming coral sun slunk from view.
At summer's end, that other stain
Would come, with its warm, dark stickiness.
"My little girl is a grown-up woman now,"
My mother would fuss, crying. What did I
Know then of stickiness—except for the grit
Of sand caked to Coppertone-coated
Skin, of ocean salt baked into sun-painted hair?
I knew of the damp, slowing confinement of Florida
Air, of geography's limits, my need
To speed things up, that would
In time transport me to a cold, fast
Place to finesse the art of bundling up,
Of layering. I was a girl still,
Curving and watchful but trusting the water,
Tucking up one leg, wading, all folded in.

ORANGES

The cool juice drips loose on our fingers.
At breakfast in the garden, as the sweet breath
Of orange blossoms mingles with the waft
Of wild creamy tea roses, nodding their silky
Heads at us in approval, and the green baby lemons,
Hanging from the tree like gumdrops, rustle against
Their lax shelter of leaves, I notice those
Hairs on your chest that have suddenly turned silver.
Winking, you slide your orange wedge entirely
Into your mouth, then flash me a fiery orange-peel smile.

Fast on the freeway, outside the groves, we passed
A bumpety flatbed truck that owned the road
With its cargo—three car lengths of oranges,
Looking so puckish, so ready to tumble, we couldn't
Stop smiling at them, thousands of flaming suns.
Hours later, from our private perch overlooking
The Palisades, with the warmth of your arm
Around me and the sun settling its vast silver quilt
On the ocean's skin, you told me that, although
You have turned thirty-nine, you still *feel* young.
We have only a short ride on that truck, my love,
A bouncy ride on the truck. Feeding each other, we
Build up the blood and its vessels, sweeten the earth.

LEVITATION

My mother's eyes, pooling over, lingered
Upon mine, shining my tiny
Face, floating in place, on their
Surfaces, fighting to lift me above
The dark weight within.
The mirrors were blindfolded,
Hung with a draping of white sheets,
As if eyes could deny their
Awareness of solids, of mists,
The invisible paint box of dreams.
I stared at my mother with the grayness
Of a dense-packed cloud, choking, ready
To drown. "Daddy has died," she finally
Said. "Do you know what that means?"

My chin reached the windowsill. I fixed
On the sky, on a white place beyond the sky.
The ceiling, a far lid pitched by the winds,
Shifted. The front yard remained laced
With snow, the tree empty of leaves, but
My feet lost the floor and I drifted
Like dust to a place too minute
To be seen. It was then I came to know
The meaning of gravity. I plunged
Myself down. There they waited
At attention in the closet, racks of them,
Polished to a sheen. Knotted
In the blackest and bulkiest oxfords,
I scuffled from room to room. I would need
My father's shoes for the rest of my life.

∾

Starting at the curtained bureau by the window,
I stripped all the mirrors. I knew
What I'd see. It's what
I see now when I stand barefoot, floating,
By the steamy glass of the medicine
Cabinet, holding the porcelain
Mooring of the sink, holding on. I see
His eyes, including the wandering one,
The eye I work so hard to compensate for,
The estate that skews all physical
Boundaries so I can never gauge
Exactly where I am. I trip. I get hit.
It is an eye with a will of its own, an eye
That drifts.

STOREHOUSE FOR ANGELS

Rockefeller Center

On the underground shopping concourse, possessed
By a sense of mission, dashing along, I had passed
That cool swath of mirrored wall hundreds of times,
Ignoring my image, a blurred flutter of wings,
On the periphery. But today my reflection halted.
The permanent wall gave way, to reveal
A cramped room lush with lacy, white wire sculptures
Looming eight feet each, a thicket of halos and wings
Piled in tiers to the ceiling, chins tipped up
And arms uplifted, awaiting their moment, their golden
Holiday place amid the spangled lights and mist of snowflakes
Dusting the garden, waiting, as if for the first time, to be seen.

I stood transfixed, having learned where the angels live,
Hidden sentinels carrying on their quiet business
Based behind mirrors. They're there every morning,
Peering out from the medicine cabinet, as we drag a razor
Against our face or, so skilled at defining, we flick
A mascara wand and glide on lipstick. Framed in the foyer,
The youngest among them pressing their noses to the glass,
They send forth a sunbath of approval, regarding us
At full length. We see them most clearly in the eyes
Of loved ones. But any shiny surface will do.
A spoon, a metallic button, a puddle, will laud your own
Particular beauty. Listen. You can hear the brass trumpets.

BABY TALK

For my nephew, Daniel

Your ardent shriek pierces the air, a giddy blast
That lifts you to uncharted reaches. Delighted
With this new skill, you wiggle your whole body
And grin, entreating me to join you, eagerly
Poised to shriek again. As always, I answer
In singsong, in a high, squeaky voice, as if dazed
On helium. The octave emerges, unbidden,
By instinct, the same way a nursing mother, hearing
Somebody else's baby scream, will find she leaks.

Just like an adult, you want to shove everything
Into your mouth. Right now, it's my knobby mountain
Of knee. You have no teeth yet, so you smack your lips
And investigate with your gums, gnawing along
The thin, salty skin, which gives up nothing. You've
Established you're hungry. About to pout, you finally
Raise your heavy head. Your deep eyes hold me and say,
"I know you'd do anything for me." Of course, you're
Correct. That's what love is. It's hearing the high notes.

Sometimes they're so high, no one can hear them
Except the two of us. They are what wakes us,
A benevolent siren song that travels in trills
And whistles across the miles, or leaps between
Two sets of eyes, as tuneful and complete as whalespeak.
Whenever you listen, this sound will sing to you.
You already know this, just as you knew the entire
Range of your mother's voice when, so very
Pleased, you discovered your fingers, in the womb.

THE SPELLING CHAMPION

The letters would flash, black and crisp,
On a white projection screen displayed
On demand on the stage inside my forehead.
The words emerged earlier than the writer's
Callus, the cushiony bump that would serve
As a pencil rest, a popped-up development,
Curious at first, like the earlier sister,
Who had arrived one day squally and bald,
Yet was quickly accepted, with a child's
Shrug and egocentric sight, as part of my life.

In front of the chalkboard, ever the teacher's
Favorite, I'd fling forth words, savoring
Their surfaces, flavor on the tongue, each letter's
Specificity and texture, while all my classmates
Would stumble on the obvious, allowing me
To stand, the winner, alone. Knowing words
Defined me more than the pencil that slid
Into place as an extra digit, spelled me
As much as the shape of my five-headed family,
The shape of my hand. How cooperative,

How kind, words seemed to be, until the nurse,
Releasing the respirator nozzle from my sister's
Face, as if removing a vacuum cleaner's
Ridged suction hose from its bag, pronounced
The patient "expired" and I lost all speech.
I knew the word: E-X-P-I-R-E-D, but
Could not comprehend this usage. "Time,"
Announced the suited official at the county bee.
As the microphone whined with feedback,

I covered my mouth, reeling, spilling over
With the unspoken, with what the eyes,
Which see things once and always remember,
Don't want to repeat. It's not
A practical skill, to spell, not if you can't
Communicate meaning, not if your central
Finger, the tough one that taught you
To write, is stolen from your hand.

HEALING DIRT

El Santuario de Chimayó, Chimayó, New Mexico

When the sun-hardened skin of adobe
Cracks, the women replaster the walls,
Scooping palmfuls of the cool, clumpy
Mud out of the wheelbarrows, spreading
It slowly, inch by inch, into a fine paste
With the fingertips, sealing the surface,
The human imprint always providing
A rounded edge. Inside the church, recessed
In the soft dirt floor to the left
Of the altar, lies the shallow
Pit, small as a manhole, shadowed
With pebbly clefts and creases,
Where kneeling pilgrims are troweling
Mounds of holy dirt into plastic bags.

Surrounded by dozens of lace-veiled saint
Dolls, dressed in pink and orange satin, draped
With the crucifix, cushioned on the shelves
By puffy clusters of fragrant flowers,
I quickly pick up a pinch of the powdery
Earth for good luck, rub it into my hands,
Letting it settle a network along the grooves.
Bunched up on the wall is the lineup
Of crutches, discards arranged
Like a burgeoning family, large to small.
A crayoned portrait of Christ, posted
With hundreds of notes, pictures, news clips,
Appeals: "Lord, please love us and bless us,
The way you love our granddaughter Amy,
Who has been in your care since her car
Accident three years ago." The littlest
Crutches, giant wishbones, speak
Of a child's first solo steps. *"Ven acá,"*
His mother, crouching, extending her arms
Streaked with the red dirt, whispered.
The dirt-smeared boy, absorbing the voice

He required like milk or warmth or breathing,
Hesitated, biting his lip, then stumbled
Across the vast three feet to his mother's
Arms. A circle of skeptics, bewilderedly
Cheering, unable to check their tears,
Applauded. "I have prepared him his entire
Life for this moment," the mother said.

Outside, the women are laughing, singing,
Patting down the walls. I sit in the front
Pew, next to a carved oak crucifix,
Chest high, delivered past craggy mesas
Strapped to a man's back, as if
The strength to walk were merely an act
Of devotion, a matter of will, carried
150 miles on foot from Grants to Chimayó,
A month's trip, in thanks for a son
Returned from Vietnam intact.
Before me, bone thin, wooden, each
Bloody seepage painted with care,
Is the Spanish Christ. I know this face,
This work, the dark curly beard,
The black-rimmed downcast
Sorrowful eyes. Although my hands
Are dusty, I have no choice—I drop
My face to my hands, until the voices
Outside rise with the jumpy beat
Of summer's pride: "¡Para bailar la Bamba!"
"La Bamba" lures me to the light,
To the yellow-blue sea of sky
So embracingly bright you can press
Yourself to it, possess it, from this
Hilled elevation, so close to the clouds.
"Una poca de gracia," the women sing—
With a little grace, with a little grace—
While the mud, shaping and smoothing
The wounded walls, bakes dry.

FISHERMAN

A dull light flickers
From the point.
The horn moans,
Water laps the pier.
You scoop me up
In the fog that conceals
The sea, the moon,
All trace of the town.
In the night's
Cloud, I let you
Nudge this seashell
Open, find
A pearl.

TOILETTE

She lifts the white, lace nightgown
Over her head, waits for hot
Water to flow into the basin.
The billowing curtain sheer, tulip appliquéd,
Rises with the breeze, revealing
The dogwood's veil of ivory blossoms,
Each with its nubby green core,
Soft-claw edges dipped in mauve.
She washes her face, slides
The washcloth along her armpits,
Between her legs, rinses.
A rush-hour traffic report—
Stalled tractor trailer, half-mile backup—
Radios faintly from the bedroom
Across the yard. She brushes her teeth,
Inserts a contact lens, blinks,
Readies the next one, when an arm
Encircles her waist, a scratchy
Face rests in the curve
At the base of her neck.
Cut off by the mirror, her index
Finger holds out the clear,
Waiting lens to the light
Like a sacrifice. A tiny, malleable cup,
It adheres, balances, preens.
It knows it's been cleansed,
That after its nightly soak—eight
Free-floating hours lazing in saline,
On wave after wave of dreams—
It offers, with transparent
Pleasure, the power to see.

TWO

RESPONSE TO A READING

For Li-Young Lee

In two of your poems you called that central
Passage of womanhood a wound,
Instead of a curtain guarding a silken
Trail of sighs. How many men,
Upon regarding such beauty, helplessly
Touching it, recklessly needing
To enter its warmth again and again,
Have assumed it embodies their own ache
Of absence, the personal
Gash that has punished their lives.
So endowed of anatomy, any woman
Who has been loved
Knows that her tenderest blush
Of tissue is a luxe burden of have.
Although it bleeds, this is only to cleanse,
To prepare yet another nesting for love.
It is not a wound, friend.
It is a home for you.
It is a way into the world.

JUNE 1978: SILVER ANNIVERSARY

June in San Juan, '53, the hum
Of the air conditioner. You shyly emerge
From the bathroom wearing your blue
Negligee. His watch sits on the nightstand.
He still wears his trousers. He steps
Toward you, tells you, "You are beautiful."
Your throat swells. This is finally
Yours. You press your full weight
Against him. Neither of you speak.

Years pass, seven. Closed in the dark
Of a white room, you collapse
In the hole of his silent chest,
Into a sunken pillow of ribs,
Wailing at the plastic tubes secured
To all his entrances and exits, at the doctor
Gripping your shoulder with his antiseptic
Hand, at the nurses bristling back and forth
Outside the door in cushioned shoes,

So far away from the briny
Bath of the ocean air, wet sand,
From a strapless dress, a gardenia corsage,
Champagne, pretending about your age,
From a week lying sunburnt
On the fresh bleached sheets
Of a hotel bed, your face
To the face of the man beside you,
Believing love was the greatest power.

INHERITANCE

Father,
In your bones
In this ground
I will always have
A house.

I reach from afar,
But for now I must
Only live
In the gardens,
Your first flower.

FOR MY MOTHER

I sharpen more and more to your
Likeness every year, your mirror
In height, autonomous
Flying cloud of hair,
In torso, curve of the leg,
In high-arched, prim, meticulous
Feet. I watch my aging face,
In a speeding time lapse,
Become yours. Notice the eyes,
Their heavy inherited sadness,
The inertia that sags the cheeks,
The sense of limits that sets
The grooves along the mouth.
Grip my hand.
Let me show you the way
To revolt against what
We are born to,
To bash through the walls,
To burn a warning torch
In the darkness,
To leave home.

THE DIORAMA

After twenty-five years it is faded, rather
As we are—the Japanese teahouse we fashioned
With satin-kimonoed dolls that fit
In the dip of a child's palm, rice bowls
Balancing toothpick bits for chopsticks,
The miniature English tea set—saucers, cups,
A sugar bowl, and a creamer. Authenticity
Was not our intent here. We used what we had
And built a house in the way we imagined it,
A mother and daughter side by side,
At a time when a mother shapes the walls
Of a daughter's universe, before a girl,
Without need for ceremony, ventures
Out to a world of her own. You saved
The world we had built in a box
In the way you have stayed in the house
Of my childhood, a faded
House you have never maintained yet never
Left, the same way you mothered your children
Once we had outgrown the diorama, once no
Room left any doubt your marriage had died.

When you set out the box, you brought back
A house so vivid that, not long after,
When I spotted a woman who so resembled you,
Except for her eyes, as blue and open as skylights,
Except for the dance in her face when she smiled,
I thought she could be you. I even
Introduced myself, but of course
There was nothing to say. She was
Not you. Your eyes are hazel. And Japan
Is not an imagined place but a real land,
Of compact, fuel-conservative cars, of stunted
Trees, carefully pruned and bound
By a strict definition of beauty, cultivated
In planters. Japan is a land of green tea.

MAN WITH PICTURE FRAME

90th and Third, NYC

We almost missed him, although his face,
As blunt as a busy Picasso, all shifting
Planes, was wedged in a picture frame.
We almost missed him, the way one can stop
Seeing hunched-over bodies along the street
Or a favorite picture above the sofa
In the living room, so familiar it seems
Invisible, until it has drifted askew
Or been removed. "If only he had something
More contemporary," my companion offered.
The man in the frame extended his crushed
Paper coffee cup, fingers hugging its Greek
Pillars and statues, white and blue.
"Spare any change?" he asked. I brought
Forth a quarter. His eyes, brilliant, said
I am a masterpiece. This is where I live.

SEIZURE

You spoke in a language only you could imagine
Or fathom: "I have to go blankus the eptor"—
Your singsong cadence and syntax making sense.
So this was what it meant, talking in tongues.
You hadn't forewarned me, the evening
Of our first coupling, that this sometimes happens
In your sleep. You awoke with a growl, unable
To hear or see, your whole body stiffened,
Shaking as if invaders had fixed on
Evicting you from your skin, gasping
As if in the last tremors of life.
I thought I had lost you.
Yet soon you emerged from this darkness,
Consumed by a foreign speech. When you finally
Awakened, every muscle sore, exhausted,
You stammered "I'm sorry," a rush of soft sounds
Echoing, trailing off. Profoundly embarrassed,
You lacked any recollection of what had passed.
Seizure: Needing sleep, you drifted off,
Holding me to you. I didn't dream that night,
In some strange tongue or any other.
Over the distance, I rested
The flesh of me next to the field of you,
The entire hidden field, sparking and rumbling.

ARTIFICIAL BREATHING

The hardest part, in the beginning, is getting down,
In spite of the weights at your waist, the aluminum
Armor guarding the ration of atmosphere
Harnessed to your back. The trick is to exhale
Deeply, knowing the heavy sea is set
To swallow you, that it will pound its bulk
To your ears, that you must shove it back
With your breath, pinching your nose so the blast
Tunnels up through your ears and keeps
The pressures equal. But once you are down,
Accepted by the cushion of the sea, by the salt
That keeps you lifted, gliding at eye level
With masses of shimmering yellow jacks,
And, shier, a fiery sky-blue, opalescent wrasse,
Suspended in a shifting Tiffany case of the deep,
You kick from the hip, a subtle effort, using
Your fins plus a conscious pacing of the lungs—
Inhaling more fully to rise, relying on
Exhales to fall—to carefully place you.
The object is neutral buoyancy: to neither dip
Nor climb without intention, but rather to hover,
To pause and remain neutral, at any given depth.
Mastering buoyancy is diving's most elusive task.

The sound of your breathing swirls in your ears
Like the surf's crash and retreat. Underwater,
Time always swims more swiftly than you do.
Checking your gauge, you confirm you have only
So much air. As a child you would test
Your lungs, you and your sister, racing to make
The length of the pool on one breath, then soaring
To break the surface, hearts thumping, chests
Swelling with air. But sometimes there is no
Surface. Sometimes there's only the deep,
That sea where your sister was, beautiful swimmer,
Drowned not by a watery absence of air

But by blood in the brain, brain-dead
On a respirator, pumping her chest up and down
With its loud wheezing: breath funneling into her,
Forced out. Your teeth clench your regulator,
The rubber mouthpiece and hose connecting you
To your air. You stare at the reef,
This risky world that you visit,
So beautiful, achingly beautiful. You start
To ascend, because you are running out of air.

STARFISH CAST ASHORE

We awoke to a sea that had such little glint. The weight
Of the rain had dulled the waves to a hammered pewter.
Wrung out and pale pearl gray, the sky had quieted.
So we headed barefoot, across the damp, packed
Sand, to the churning edge, to the eternal
Thunder and chase, to find the shore littered for miles
With miniature starfish, strands and mounds of tawny
Pinwheels an inch across. I picked up two of them,
Ran a finger along their lank, bristly limbs. No longer alive.

The sea hit our feet. On the evening we met, overriding
The crush and the din in the dim light of a party, you
Told me you were adopted. "You don't know what it's like
To feel abandoned," you confided just weeks later
With a trace of pride, as if but a chosen few could cradle
A loss. "Hold me," you'd ask, eagerly rushing in close
Before heeding a greater force and retreating again,
Like the tide. You picked up your own pair of starfish, finally,
Nearly an hour into our walk. "They're pretty," you admitted,
Carefully redepositing them on the sand. I had pocketed mine.

FOUND OBJECTS

I pick up the blue-striped curlicue jacket
Of a lost mollusk. My heels sink
In the sand, soggy from the runaway
Foam that slaps and slides forward again.
I pocket the shell, a lone white gull feather,
Reject trails of raggedy black brittle
Crab pincers, a grit-crusted raspberry
Dannon container, a child's chewed-up rubber thong.

Not much selection against this sundown, silvery
Cloud-shingled sky. None of the cowries—whorls
And dips and nodules, creamy white and brown—
None of the turrets, tritons, turkey wings,
That with summer's salvation
From book strap and pencil case,
Beginning with the class-wide whoop
At the final bell, so defined my life.

"She can swim, my little one, watch her swim,"
My grandmother boomed to her inner-tubed
Mah-jongg cronies, clustered around like barnacles
To a pier. Our tube was snug—for me,
My grandmother, my grandmother's breasts.
I'd slither out, a frolicking porpoise arcing up
And under and up, return to kisses and freckled,
Leathery-skinned applause. A school of white-capped
Inner tubes, we'd paddle back to shore.
Stalking the edge, I'd sift through seaweed,
Pail in hand, collecting shells.

At a splintery picnic table shaded by an umbrella
Under the palms, my grandfather played pinochle.
I'd sidle up to him. Always, he'd wink, snap
Forward his lower denture with his tongue,
Evoking my practiced yelp. The others would chortle
And wheeze and ask me to marry them. I'd sit

Quietly, stacking towers of tottering chips.
After the game, two sweat-drenched sleepwalkers,
We'd head for the luncheonette, order
My grandfather's cherry soda and my butter-pecan
Cone, numbing cold against the socketed gap
Where I waited for top teeth. A revived windup
Toy, I'd ride right and left on the red vinyl stool.

I'd sit in the tub on top of a half-inch-high
Accumulation of beach, previously plastered to me,
Inside my suit, in the most unlikely places.
The aroma of pot roast mingled with Dial,
Breck, Vitalis, Listerine, as my grandmother,
The aproned Ethel Merman of West Bahama Drive,
Bellowed a coloratura "Seventy-six Trombones"
And dashed more paprika into the pot.
My grandfather snoozed in front of the television,
The *Hollywood Sun-Tatler* on his lap.
Dinner over, on the back porch, against
A streaky cobalt and apricot sky,
The scent of gardenias and ripening mangoes,
And the sputtering putt-putt-putt of the sprinklers,
The three of us praised and sorted shells.

On a different beach, at the close of a day,
I still scavenge the shore, combing the sand
For what has been taken away, and what has been
Tossed back, looking to the sea
For a salt-sticky seven-year-old—honey tanned,
Her corkscrew ponytails wagging—a bikinied
Torpedo crashing into the water
With a wild-splatter belly-flop splash,
Walking à la handstand, diving
Under a wave, so as not to be
Tumbled to shore, rising to the surface
To wait for the next breaker, bobbing.

MIRAMAR

My grandfather takes out his teeth
By the light of a candle.
At dawn he had cranked
Shut the awnings.
I cuddle up under the covers
Next to my transistor radio.
School has been canceled, winds
Are 60 miles per hour, branches
Crack off the mango tree,
Rain, like a riot of nails,
Pellets the house.
A single clankety trash can
Tumbles down the road.
The dark is opaque, thick.
The dampness hovers
Batlike over my head.
I climb out of bed, step
On bath towels lining the floors
In case of flooding, pad
To the front door,
Lean against it.
Rainwater dribbles in
At the cracks.
I cup my hands
Around the cool metal doorknob.
Grandfather kicks in his sleep
As he speeds through the marsh,
Fleeing from a snap-jawed
Alligator glaring
At the pink of his heels
Through hard golden eyes.

SOLVED IN SLEEP

It is all solved in sleep,
The way a mother sates
A suckling infant's lips.
Even these rocks I carry
Serve as a decent bed.
I set them out in the dry clearing,
Leaving the twigs where they lie,
As always. Not much wind.
No moon. The sounds are coming:
Little fur in the dirt. Soon
The pictures, the billows.
Dead leaves ruffle my face
Like a soft gauze curtain.
I am covered. What
I need to know is
Dense, pliant, dark.

THREE

THE KEEPER OF LIGHT

The little one listens but never reveals
What she knows. By day she controls the light
That filters across the roofs, through
Trees, on furrows of plaintive faces.
She wakes up alone and unlocks
Cabinets of light, allots the portions
Strictly, patiently hears requests
For additional rays. What a job.
She has to be careful. Not long ago,
In a moment of passion, she almost
Gave away the whole reserve. Phones
Incessantly ring. Amazing, someone
Thanks her for light. She has to hang up.
Her cheeks are ballooning, deflating,
As if she were some nervous fish.
She scoots in the broom closet, fits
On the funnel. Her face is beaming.
She targets the freshly erupting supply
Into a spare metal cashbox, hides it
Under newspapers in her desk.
No one has noticed. Flushed,
She sorts through the mail,
Coos a wilted sigh. So many tasks,
Yet the barest assistance.
When she leaves, later, again,
She will dot the night, star by star.

TYPING IN THE NUDE

It could be our still life: five o'clock sun
On a basket of lemons, cups cold with breakfast
Coffee, newspapers, bills, old messages, wax
On the tablecloth, shadows in the folds.

You trace an outline. I am upstairs, typing,
While you set out your oils and brushes, painting
For the first time in years. I write a fiction
In which we are both main characters. Restive,

I move away. You get a new job, wish you could
Fall in love, picture me as always typing, imagine
Portraits of drape-hidden women never stilled
On a canvas, of beauty never constant in a frame.

A POET'S MUSEUM

It is one of the first tenets of drawing:
That space is a shape, dense
With as much substance as objects.
That absence, the question that hugs
The objects, has contours that can be
Delineated and shaded. You step next
To the textured black-purple night
Of the painting before you, to the white
Pellets of starlight embossed on their base.
A uniformed guard poses near the archway. Light,
Through banks of bare, narrow windows, douses the room.

At times, with a violence, you find you must handle
The materials, must collide all your fate
Into that soft unknown and color
The space. Perhaps you also yearn to have
Your skin against skin of someone who is distant.
With appropriate tools you can literally take
The space between objects into your hands —
Define it, perfect it — then display it
On a wall in one of the well-lit rooms
Of your past and your present, where it will
Preside on permanent view, enfolding the light.

THE KINESTHETIC OBSERVER

For the Boston Ballet

We called *The Nutcracker* "The Ballbuster"—
The Sugar Plum Fairy and swarms
Of tulle-twirling dancers glissading
Across the stage, their ice-pink
Stiff-tipped slippers packing
Knobby, bleeding corns on every toe.
Our blitz of New England: thirty shows
In three weeks. I claimed
A tenth-row-center, tattered velvet
Seat at dress rehearsal, the grande-dame
Ragged rococo Music Hall to myself.
I had earned this command performance—
The jangling bank of auxiliary
Phones removed, the run sold out.
The orchestra proffered its bleeps
And blurts in preparation, hushed,
Sprung by the maestro's
Sweep of baton, surged.
A servant possessed, I wore my
Poverty like a shield. I worked for art.

Early that evening, thousands of bug-eyed
Children craned to extend their view.
"I hope there'll be lions in this show,"
Murmured the wriggling girl behind me.
"Are they playing tag?" inquired
A squeak-voiced boy across the way.
I sat in an aisle press seat,
Inaugurated wild applause
With each orbit of leaps,
Dizzying spin, whenever a tiaraed,
Sequin-tutued, teeth-clenched smiling
Ballerina, straight and sharp
As if plucked from a jewel box,

Relinquished the grip
Of her cavalier's anchoring hand
And, poised in arabesque, allied
With the flight of the violins,
Floated like a bloom
On the stem of that lone
Pointed foot, supported by air.

Finale over, the dancers and stagehands
Departed, the audience disappeared,
An internal pilot propelled me
Against all rules
To the footlit lip of the stage.
Absent of people, of sound, the theater
Retained a hulking physical presence,
An almost audible, vibrating, charged,
Enveloping tone, that rose from the hollows
Of the worn scarlet seats, lifted
My arms, my chest, my heels, carried
Me weightlessly beyond my limited frame,
Higher and higher, to a place where,
At twenty-two, with little sense
Of time, or death, or memory,
I had witnessed the means
To approximate beauty,
Endlessly reaching
On pointe.

THE BLIND SPOT

I.
When you learn how to drive later in life,
Primed by a heightened sense of the roadway's
Panorama, by a picture of time as an ongoing
History that stretches and shifts, you know
You can lapse, lost in a moment's glance
The wrong way, and ram into anyone,
That any driver at random can slam into you.
You have mastered the critical lesson:
Objects in mirror are closer than they appear,
A warning meant to be taught and tested
In youth. If this should be missed, you may lack
Perspective when you are plunked in a foreign
Place, let's say a college campus in Boston,
The autumn of 1972. A woman on your floor—for you
Are now considered a woman and not a girl—keeps
Quoting a new magazine called *Ms.* On the cover
Is Wonder Woman. Students in Indian cotton
Are walking barefoot in Kenmore Square.

II.
You are taking the Pill, because the new rule
Is that you are entitled to pleasure, because
The sensations you have yet to experience
Now seem as much of your course work
As Hegel and Yeats. And there is a ride board,
A full-wall collage of flaps tacked up on a map,
A span from ocean to ocean, a legion of students
Needing to travel someplace, students willing to drive.
You take home some numbers, and soon you are on the road
To Baltimore, two hours in, when the driver—so polite
When it came to explaining why other riders had canceled—
Sets down a glinty knife with a pearlized handle
Beside the gearshift, touches an index finger
To your lips, then pinches them, pinching your voice:
A numb lump crouched in your throat, it refuses

To come out. Later, you will not recall any
Names of exits or in which towns you paused.
All you will know is hours and hours of highway.

III.
He uses the knife, carving a hole in your chest
Precisely. You are too young to recognize
What it is he has taken, that shadowy form.
Cast aside, it kneels beside you, observing
In horror, wanting to assist your corpus, to bury
That knife in the eye of the driver. At the least,
To scream or to hit. You obey all instructions.
At one point you vomit, your mouth unprepared
For the fullness and pressure, the sharpness
Of flavor. He yanks back your hair with his fist
So the roots ache, arcing your neck, each delicate
Bone of it, arcing the axis, the twiggy brace
On which the head pivots, and the atlas, the tiny
Rock that carries the skull, bones you had never
Before given thought to, bones you had always
Assumed were yours. Still tugging your hair, he
Scoops up your sludge in his palm, forms a lid
From your nostrils to chin. You know you
Have no alternative. "Swallow it," he insists.

IV.
Slowed to a sleepwalk, a primitive muscle memory,
You go through the motions of a life. The officer
Closes the door and, sipping coffee, cuts you off
Only a few sentences in. "Now that was your
Mistake," he says in a timbre tired and soft.
You attempt to continue, but he interrupts you.
"That was your mistake," he says again. You visit
The doctor, who tells you your cervix is so raw
It has to be cauterized, to bring on a scab to heal it.
You hardly hear him, see even less, and yet a flavor

Remains in your mouth like a stale lozenge, in spite
Of the dozens of brushings, the easy way that
Your gums bleed. It lingers for weeks—the flavor
Of semen. You cannot get rid of it, until the moment
You lose what is left of your senses—smell, hearing,
Touch. You have stepped from the elevator. Waiting
In front of the door to your dorm room, the driver
Is smiling, his hands wound around a bouquet of flowers.

V.
Almost the extent of another girlhood later, you stare
At the road ahead, then up at the mirror. All
Looks fine. Yet your hands clutch the steering wheel
As if it could steal you to places you have no
Desire to find. You check past your shoulder.
That's when you notice, floating, your own
Lost face, that scarred angel part of you.
Having hovered for years, it is prepared to wait
More years, as many years as you need. It waits
For your signal, for the moment you know
You are ready to claim that open space, to focus
Directly on what is behind you, ready to merge.

SAUSALITO FERRY

The fog hangs on the hills,
Eclipsing all but the edge of the bridge,
A mile-high woolly ghost, hugging
Our crossing on three sides, expanding
With each slumbery inhale,
Advancing with each release.
Our ferry departs
From the rusted hills, from the elegant
Bridge we have faith exists.
The sun litters diamonds
On top of the blue-green bay.
Scores of sailboats, slivers
Of crescents, list in the wind
As we enter the fog layer, clasping
The deck's chilly railing, wrapped
In the vapory damp,
Able to see one another
Vaguely, nothing more.
We know what to expect now.
Most of us wait for the dock beyond,
A wavering choice. Many
Are lifted out of their skin,
Carried by gulls, flap-weary, scrawking
At the cumbrous weight of human mist.
It is a temptation, this rolling
And resting upon the sea. I try
To ignore it. On a steep-angled
Bus that skitters up
Powell Street, my breath
Clouds the glass.

ISLAND TIME

As the afternoon fades, the sea pulls
Pigment out of the sky, deepens
To a sleepy twilight. Fanning yourself,
You wait for the rumbling jitney, now
An hour late. "Has the schedule changed?"
You query the driver, who snaps
His head back, laughing, flashing
A rosy throat and six gold teeth.
He tips you his skipper's cap.
"You just sit down," he says,
"And take it cool until she comes.
You just sit down, and take it cool"—
A chant that bounces in your blood
All the way home, as you loll
Low-slung in the hammock, a shifting
Airborne skiff overlooking the rocky
Shore. At noon a ruckus
Of yellow-pinstriped miniature
Fish, their fretwork of bones exposed,
Had scurried across your ankles
As you waded in. Sinking to shoulder
Level, you could see the moons
Of your toenails. The surface
Burned with the sun's rippling trim.

You bolt up when thunder crackles.
In the corner of the open-air hut,
A cat-size iguana, jutting its chin out,
Fixes its gaze on a circle of leaves
Chasing its tail on the dirt floor,
Darts back to the bushes,

As the heavens release a speeding
Bomb-blast black tornado, clasped
To the clouds, churning to feed
Its maker, sucking up fighting
Whitecaps at the horizon. Tilted,
This column of heat
Hoards as much of the sea as it can,
Holding you spellbound for perhaps
Twenty minutes—you wear no watch—
Until it disintegrates, slowly,
Into a wisp.

EVERGLADES AND MANGOES

Its arrowhead snout, fringed with teeth, was bound
By only a slim housing of rubber band.
"Don't be afraid. It won't hurt you—take it,"
Said the shirtless man holding out the still baby
Alligator, breathing so deeply, in lingering waves,
Eyeing me with the fire of the noonday sun.
One runnel of sweat slid down my back as I clutched
The lizard around its middle, unexpectedly
Warm and soft, a complex of slithery beauty, such
Silent potential, small heart thumping against my hands.

Back on the trail, I gaze at a lone heron wading—swan
On stilts. Bussed by a thin breeze, the saw grass
Barely bristles while a turtle the size of a silver dollar,
As green and lit from within as a spring leaf, shuffles out
Onto the path, beside my feet. I know now that cold-blooded
Means a reptile can raise or lower its body temperature
By taking its weight to hotter or cooler surroundings.
On island banks in the river of grass, hundreds of gators
Doze in clumps, overlapped like napping puppies,
Most of them half dunked in the tepid marsh. Clever,

How nature provides such adaptations, how a person
Can endure being locked in the jaws of an animal,
Wrestle with adrenaline strength for each draft of air,
Feel blades of teeth break the skin, the soft flesh
Tear, yet emerge with a heart that continues
To pump, an onrush of fever that, over time, clears.
And the past may persist but is met by a turtle on the path,
By the smile of a child you adore so fully, he makes you the sky
That embraces the earth, by the taste of a ripened mango,
Best once it has fallen from the tree, blushing and bruised.

BADGE

A hard yellow badge is carved
In my forehead: *Jude,*
As plain as Asian eyes, as
African color and hair,
As plain as a mouth
Of the earth
Accepting a tumble
Of bones, bodies
Shrunken to bones,
Crushing bones, a tangle
Of two hundred corpses
Kissing in a mouth,
My mouth. My forehead,
A heritage, a tombstone lit
By six points of fire.

TREES

Jerusalem

The spade hits a stone. And the stone, asleep
In this spot for centuries, will not be moved.
So I carry the two baby shoots, cupping
Each by its bundle of roots, a few feet away,
Then dig in a softer place, where the dirt
And smaller stones give easily. Gathering
The graveled soil with my hands, tamping it down,
I set these trees into the earth, the home
Where I put you, Father, and put you,
Sister. I plant two foot-high cypresses
In your names, gardening a barren
Hill in the family plot, the land of Abraham.

They join acres of forests planted tree by tree,
Until 200 million were planted, and a people
Who reclaimed a desert, their hands in the soil.
How much wandering, and how many stones
In the path, before we can stand on the land
We were promised, before we succumb to the land
As stones ourselves. Yet stands of our trees,
Limbs shifting in the breeze, keep on breathing.
I plant trees among stones, and after I leave,
Each raises its dusty face to feed on the sunlight,
To exhale what's unseen, the element that gives
Us the chance to wake and dance, and grieve.

ELEVATION BESIDE THE DEAD SEA

In the midday heat, the pilgrims from Kenya
Were singing "Amazing Grace" in Swahili
As the cable car drifted us down from the desert
Mountaintop, from the fortress that hovers above
A sunken sea so clouded with salts
It sustains no life. The thousand Zealots
Who had thrived here for seven years, trapped
By the final siege, took knives to themselves — each
Husband slashing the tense, familiar flesh
Of his wife and children, then presenting
His throat to an executioner, one of ten selected
By lots, who, done with the blood, designated
A last killer, to slay them and himself — rather than
Bow to slavery under the Romans. Preserved
In the cinnamon dust, along with the potsherds,
Cisterns and frescoes, is the synagogue,
Its bleached stone benches facing Jerusalem.

I could have raced down Masada's worn, snaking path
With the fire of my tour mates, but I needed
The ease of the cable car, its slow pulley
Floating me to the base. I had already run from the top
To the scuffed bottom stones of too many such
Mountains, hurtled my way to the living with barely
A sense of the vista, an athlete of loss. I stared
At the sun searing the sky as I clung
To a handrail, my mind flitting to the face
Of the pretty young man, born when I was a teenager,
Whose gaze had tempted me. I shook my head, forgiving
Of all my foolishness. "It's only because you need
To feel loved," I said to myself. It was then, so
Matter-of-factly, out of the mountain, the sizzling sky,
A steady voice entered and claimed my body,
Alerted my every nerve, halted my breath to hold me
Still, insisting I listen. "You *are* loved," it said.
It was exactly 1:00 P.M. The Kenyans were singing.

∾

A powdery dust encases my shoes. The earth
Crunches beneath my feet as I step
Through the canyon that is the heart.
At its lowest point is a body of water. I know
It will never allow me to drown. It buoys me up.

SILENT NIGHT

So your wife doesn't want you.
We stare at the tree jeweled with lights,
Which stands taller than ten of us, white star
At its pinnacle. As the skaters nearby
Fumble under the eyes of the golden Prometheus,
Clasping the fire that cost him such a price,
You tell me how your daughter insisted
At age three that the tree at her school
Was *much* bigger than the one glittering here.

Your daughter, her rosy limbs even narrower
Than your fingers, was born a decade ago
On Christmas, weighing two pounds. Laboring
For breath as she lay in the incubator,
She felt the warmth of your finger against her—
This home for your child had a hole that permitted
But one finger to fit—and she gripped it,
Held on and held with such a fist.

That Christmas, of '82, I was in the hospital too,
Waiting at the bed rail of a sister of twenty-four
Whose blood had decided to fail, flooding
Her body, which ballooned to near double
Its size, her wide eyes glazed, brain still.

This Christmas, as the skaters loop round the rink,
All laughter, you plan for divorce.
Your wife doesn't want you.
You ache like a live tree uprooted
From its earth. Your daughter seems fine now,
As does your son, although they are with you
Only a third of the week, each day on your own so long.
~

At midnight, when we rest in the dark,
The flow and sigh of our breathing
The loudest sound, and you draw me closer, we can
Almost hear the distant songs of the season—
That praise of a bright star. Like the heart's
Flame, it either gives out or endures.
It blazes a path for us. At times it can
Save us. Other times, it just drifts us to sleep,
Granting a few unbroken hours of heavenly peace.

FOUR

NIGHT VISION

We set out from the house's gold
Sockets of light, into the murky
Blackness, each footfall
A crunch on the gravel drive,
A path we have memorized.
Under a sky slurry with cloud, no
Stars, our shadows, elongated
Flat Giacomettis hand in hand,
Stilt-walk ahead of us, sink
Headfirst into the night's
Opaque pool. Colors
Fade into sharpened sounds:
Constant mower-shrill cicadas
Drown out the dark, lost green
Of the dewy grass. Past
The curved stand of trees,
The moon, pearly and round, greets
Us like a sudden spotlight, gilding
Our outlines, posing as backdrop
For our ripened silhouettes.
My eyes, adjusting, blink,
Absorb the beams of your gray
Eyes: black, two orbs of the night
Lighting a trail that will lead
To the lake, still, obsidian shiny,
Edged by the long-stemmed antenna
Heads of monochromatic
Wildflowers. Silent,
They watch us while
We stare at each other,
Our bridged, wavering image
On the water, pale and indistinct.

VETERANS MEMORIAL

It shone in the photos, a granite wingspread,
A chevroned, dark, shimmering bird
As seen from the sky. But now on the ground,
Months after his own great flight,
It is only a steady climb.
He shadows the black wall, the earth
A trajectory rising to mirror his launch
Through time. Midway, hand in his jacket
Pocket, holding the frayed white paper
With the name and date, its crosshatched
Creases as sheer as the folds
Of an overused map, he begins racing.
Stopping short downslope, he locates
The panel, a line listing '71s, a cluster of Ps,
Fingers dancing on the stone until the fire
Of particular letters carved lurches
Him backward: Errol Perkins Jr.
"*Bui!*" he shouts—"Dust!"—swiftly
Pounding the wall with his fist.
"Go back to your country," his people
Had taunted him. American. "*Bui doi*"—
Dust of life. Monster. Ugly. Child of dust.

Striking his father's name, he finds
Himself pummeling his own reflection
On the glassy surface, his wet-streaked
Face, his big-eyed, dark, American face.
58,000 dead. An army forgotten: 25,000 born.
He imagines this father, nineteen, in crisp
Khakis and oversize shiny boots,
Carefully carrying three pink, magenta-spotted
Orchids—fragile, alert, on tall stems—
Strutting up his mother's litter-strewn,
Bustling, unpaved street right before
A storm, wind whipping the palm fronds.
His fluttery mother, performing both roles

In a play she had reenacted countless
Times, portrayed each detail
About the orchids, his father's
Drum-in-the-throat laugh.
She had selected him for his laugh.
Six weeks later, stepping through swamp
Grass, one of those heavy, snug-laced
Boots touched off a land mine,
Lifting him fifteen feet in the air
With the ease of a bird's leap, the way
A gust sweeps up a scrap of paper,
Tossing him skyward to be lost
In a spray of blood, the blast
Scattering random pieces of flesh.

WHEN THE LAST CHILD LEFT

She doesn't notice how the carpet
Has faded, how the years have passed,
The house as quiet as winter.
She dusts the piano.
When the last child left,
She knew he would never return.

The pile of mail unanswered.
At the kitchen table
She tastes the familiar
Scorch of steaming tea.
The cat on her lap dozes.
Today she must mow the lawn.

She carefully unfolds a yellow
Napkin beside her saucer, spills out
The jar of baby teeth,
Grazes them with her fingertips,
Their tiny rough crowns.
Little bones, they cost her
Only a quarter, each one.

THE SACRIFICE AND THE PRAYER

The old man transfers his packages
From the display case into the freezer:
Veal chops, rump roasts, set on paper beds
Called diapers, labeled, plastic wrapped.
An apron barely soiled. How the world
Changes. In Minsk, as a boy of ten,
He slaughtered his first calf.
The soft creature wobbled against him,
Eyes as true as a looking glass,
Glistening, damp as berries in the rain.
He couldn't help crying. "Be a man," his father
Whispered. The rabbi—bent and old as a tree—
Who spoke in a booming voice but
Rarely scolded, had offered a blessing.
The boy repeated. Across the yard
The wind was flapping his mother's sheets.
He pressed the calf to his chest, slit
The jugular, blood splattered
Onto his face, the brim
Of his new black hat.
A blessing, a buckling,
A shower of blood—the power
To end life, the power to kindle it.

How the world changes. *Kineahora,*
He can't complain. Two dutiful sons, seven
Grandchildren, beautiful *kinder,* with lists
Of college degrees, "professionals,"
Hotshots—they act like they're Rockefellers!—
So many grand dreams. But what do they know?
Ach, nothing! The baby, sixteen,
She already drives a fancy car.
He wipes the counter, chuckling.
After these long years,

Now so easy to laugh.
"My kids are good to me!"
He says out loud to his chickens,
Yet to be plucked and cleaned.
And then, as if he could still behold
Her sweet, assuring face: "Essie,
You said there was always hope
In children." He hangs up
His apron, returns to the freezer
To examine the lone hooked
Carcass waiting, tomorrow's task.
And briefly he nods good night
To the work of another day.

THE PARTING

He stood outside the glass swing door
To her place of business,
Watching her wait to enter
The elevator, hoping
She would look back.
That they had said goodbye,
That he was to leave
For the other side of the country,
Seemed distant and muffled,
Like a reminder
From a voice beyond a wall.
She was forbidden,
Of his own flesh,
As kin to him, almost, as sister.
Yet she was the woman
With entry to the solemn
Soldier-child
Who stands guard
At his intimate knowledge,
The woman who had escaped
From under his skin.
That they had said goodbye—
A tentative graze of the cheek,
A hurried embrace—
Was now but the loss
Of a leaf,
A promise
That, in a matter of time, lands.
He was still holding her.
He would always
Hold her. He knew this
When she looked back.

A SISTER FAR AWAY

She sat cross-legged, studious, on the bed,
Cupping her fine-featured moon face
In her hands, watching me empty, methodically,
Each bureau drawer, pack a trunk, two
Scuffed-up suitcases, cartons of records
And books, alert for the first time
To the fact of my departure, quiet,
Awed that I would fly to a faraway place
Where I knew no one.
She had a child's smooth skin, no
Beginnings of breasts. She was the slow
Sister. I was the one in a hurry.
"I wish I could be like you," she gushed
As we sat pulsing on the edge
Of an overstuffed suitcase
To close it. Nestling my voice
To her ear, in hundreds of late-night
Calls she would plead for direction.
In time, she would always
Be lost. As adults we would never be peers.

On her first, her final, night in the hospital,
Her pale skin paler than ever, her tongue
And mouth swollen and purple
From her earlier blackout and fall,
She described the lunge of the steel drill
Boring deep in her chest for bone marrow
That afternoon. "It hurt" was all
She could whimper, her doughy face
Crumpling into folds, her eyes damp.
The newly replaced gauze patch, framed
With tape to her broken skin,
Was a spreading blossom of red. The wound

Had been seeping for hours, refusing to clot.
I dabbed Vaseline on her cracked, chapped
Lips. "I'm tired," she said to us, one arm
Hooked up to the IV, the other to plasma.
"You'd better go now. I'll see you tomorrow"—
Words that clung to us, our clothes, like moist
And cloying tropical air,
The last words we would hear her speak.

We were two curly-haired daughters
In identical dresses—fresh-pressed white
Sleeveless shifts with bunchy red-checked rosettes.
"Watch your sister, honey," our mother instructed,
Burrowing purse-wide for her fat, snapped wallet
To pay the cashier. We stood near the carts—
Our fingers locked, a leash—my sister
Launched in a jiggly six-year-old's dance,
Or startlingly silent and still,
That dreamy glaze in her eyes, gone
To that place where children go,
That shimmery, ice-blue castle
Cresting the clouds, or the friendly jungle
Where the monkeys screech in the trees,
The lion comes up to lick you like a dog.
I'd call her name softly—"Cathy"—
Reeling her in. Upturning her face, she'd
Smile, reply with guileless
Eyes that knew I would always be there,
That tiny, listening hand.

NURSING CHICKEN POX ALONE

By the hundreds, the tiny fireballs blister
And pearl on your chest and back,
Scalp, nose, the rims of your ears.
Three erupt, raising their translucent crowns,
In the wet of your gums. But the most painful
Are the red pair in the crease underneath
Your breast, silky hollows that shimmer
With rawness, a reminder
That the skin and all it encases
Are only a loan. You have never owned them.

Sleep has abandoned you for days, and you find
Yourself pleading, as if with a loved
Mate who has left you: "I need you—come back!"
The itching returns, so severe that the most
You can do is sit up in bed and rock.
For hour after hour, the night endures.
You blaze like the night sky.
Each star basks in its gassy heat.

MASTERING VERTIGO

Rio Grande Gorge Bridge, Taos, New Mexico

Heading out toward the sun, the range
Seems to stretch without end, a land
Woolly with tufts of piñon and silvery-green
Sage, providing the eye with an unimpeded sweep
Of orange, mountain-rippled raw
Horizon. The skinny six-mile road,
A taut marauder, offers no clue. Only once
I am brinked on the bridge does the chasm
Hit me: a massive gash, the land
A flesh cut to bone and sinew. Gravity
Slams the backs of my knees, tries
To drag me over the rail, down the rocky,
650-foot drop that zigzags out to a vanishing
Point, a hidden perpendicular place
Where the earth's torn loss gnaws at the sky.

As if teetering on a balance beam, crouching,
Arms extended, I stand by the central
Dividing line of the bridge, more comfortable
Dodging pickup trucks than approaching
The slatted gaps in the sidewalk's rail.
Bouncing his butt, dangling his legs off
The edge, a sun-leathered cowboy of eighty hoots
As he pinwheels his arms for his wife's Polaroid.
Traffic vibrates the bridge. I weave, praying
To the sky, the gorge, the silver
Trickle of river below me, that I not fall.

It is not a myth that Native Americans
Do not fear heights. Worshiping godliness
Rooted deep in the earth instead of afloat
In the heavens, they found it perverse
When Europeans claimed the living, sacred

Land, Mother of man, presumed to divide it.
The conquerors gave them a choice:
Accept Christ or we cut off your left foot.
At Taos Pueblo, chapel murals, lit
By a flame-blue sky empty of cloud, feature
A dark Jesus swaggering through the corn.

Returning, determined, I straddle the middle
Of the bridge and wait for the spinning
Wind to die down inside me. Stepping up
To the rail, surrounded, I allow the land to seep
Into my skin, in the same second-nature way
I admit the sun. Stepping over the air,
Trusting a foothold of nothingness, I lose
My fluid illusion of shelter, of privacy separate
From *that*. For the moment an ancient presence,
A fact larger than faith, cuts to my core.
There is only that—a crack in the crust.

LUCKY SMILE

Yielding cell from celluloid, a script for two
Refined in the mind's crevasse, Hinckley
Had fixed on that actress, her grin
In the dark—the girl he had needed to impress.
He had wanted her flowery scent on his
Pillow, the small of her back against
His hand. "Her lucky smile," he revealed
In confinement, that was the feature he liked
The best. And this young woman, a freshman
In college, who had witnessed the same scene
As we had, on the screen that we live with,
That window that brings in the world
Upon waves we can't see in the sky, saw
The president shot, shoved into the limo,
The shooter seized, the head on the pavement
Leaking, Brady flat, sunk in a puddle
Of blood, and learned, so much sooner than
Most of us, just what a bullet is, the way it can
Lodge right behind the eyes, color all that one sees,
Leave a metallic remnant of blood lingering
On the tongue, a flavor it seems one will never
Be rid of. She uses her smile now to show
How the wounded stand, how blood can be mopped,
How to bandage, each lesson in character
So we carry a heartbeat heard
As we make our way out of the theater,
Blinking at the light, at a face
That we know, at an onslaught of others
That surely we'll never know,
At the weight of the roles
We must play, almost larger than life.

SWIMMING

She tightens and dives in, has no patience
For the shallow end of the pool,
As he sits on the lounge, deposits
The half-empty tumbler
Of iced tea, condensation dripping,
Blows up the wilted pillow
Of the orange raft, his pulsing
Cheeks distended with the ache
Of obstructed air.
Urgently stirred
By a rush of the blood, she requires
This submersion, this skimming
The latticework of the bottom,
The veiny light a wavering, helical
Crosshatch imposed
On the creamiest blue
Skin, her private expanse,
A flesh that's been magnified
Ten thousand times.
She lazily kicks, wheeling
Her arms in identical ovals,
Propels herself to the surface,
The hazy swirling of light,
To air, the beyond.
The clean taste of chlorine
Addresses her lips.
He shoots cross the pool
On the raft, tumbles off, loops
His arms around her waist.
She allows him to enter her world,
As they glide together
Naked, laughing and splashing.

CONVERSATIONS DURING SLEEP

I wake with the light that outlines
The blinds and lick my lips,
My tongue thick and unfamiliar,
Woozy from its dry room.
I have been sleeping again
With my mouth open, mumbling again
Through the night. Perhaps you responded.
Then I would have answered — a conversation
Now drifted from memory, a muffled
Insistence, much like my heartbeat
Or dreaming, an impulse outside my control.
I wedge myself next to you, careful
Not to disturb you, your eyes drugged
With their thick dusting of sleep.

"I'm off to the dentist!" I once blurted,
Eyes closed, as I thrashed the mattress.
Lifting your head, you muttered, "What?"
After Robert De Niro, distended as Jake La Motta,
Had forced an index finger to each
Of my top eyeteeth, pressing
As hard as he could, harder, until
They dangled, twisting, at the root.
"There!" he had hollered before
He vanished to a pinprick, spluttering
Up toward the clouds from a swamp-edged
Parking lot in West Hollywood, Florida —
A tubby balloon whizzing up
In reverse suck. My mouth
Was a bucket of blood. I vowed,
"I have to store these teeth in milk.
That will preserve them at least an hour."
You nudged me awake. I slid my tongue
Across my top horseshoe of teeth.
"You were shouting," you whispered,
Blanketing yourself over me. "It's okay."
∾

Or, one night, trapped, power out, with the windows
Rattling, we paced through a shadowy
House in the path of a hurricane.
"We have to get out!" you insisted, your face
A pearly bulb looming in the dark.
Collecting my calm, I cupped my hands
To the ridge of your shoulders, growled,
"We can crack this lock—I know it!"
Then broke down the door to discover
My sister, sunlit, on a far-off hill, alone
On a barren horizon. A delicate breeze
Lifted the edge of her dress, a swath
Of impossible waist-length hair. She did
Not see us holding hands in the doorway.
We did not speak. Even asleep,
I knew she'd been dead for seven years.

I held off for months before I would
Sleep beside you soundly. I'd lie quietly,
Letting the hours pass, waiting for the light.
Lovemaking is private, true, but
It's not sleep, the deepest secret of all.
While your mind would be sunk
In its undercurrents, I'd listen
To you breathe, wonder if you would
Understand my need to speak in the dark.
∽

Now, as the day disappears, we coincide.
You turn out the light and curl up
Beside me to kiss me, a bridge on our journey
To sleep. "Good night," you say nightly.
I wish you the same. We both know
How easily it could be otherwise.
I settle my head at the top of your
Chest, so I can be lulled by its noisy voice,
By a world that pulses and gurgles,
Percusses, that rises
And falls. I respond in kind.

POETRY CHAPBOOK

"Does it have a spine?" the bookseller
Chided, reluctant to stock a collection
With less evident heft than its stonier kin.

"It has a thin but determined spine,
Staple-bound," I replied. "It stands
On its own. And when you open it, its mottled
White wings will carry you, high on that spine,
Across echoing, dry-river canyons riddled
With petroglyphs, beyond hidden cabins
Dotting tree-glutted mountaintops, a gray spired
City indulgent to street-corner marionettists
And blaring traffic that hugs the square,
Until it lands you, past miles of sea as subtle
As twilight, upon your doorstep, with your
Heart wanting to open its spare room
To strangers, everything crisp."

ABOUT THE AUTHOR

Michele Wolf is the author of *The Keeper of Light*, 1995 winner of the *Painted Bride Quarterly* Poetry Chapbook Series. Her poems have appeared widely in literary journals—including *Poetry, The Hudson Review,* and *Boulevard* —and anthologies, such as the award-winning *When I Am an Old Woman I Shall Wear Purple* and *I Am Becoming the Woman I've Wanted,* both from the Papier-Mâché Press. Recipient of an Anna Davidson Rosenberg Award for Poems on the Jewish Experience, she has also been awarded residency fellowships by Yaddo, the Edward F. Albee Foundation, and the Virginia Center for the Creative Arts. Raised in Florida, she was educated at Boston University and the Columbia University Graduate School of Journalism. She lives in New York City, where she works as a magazine writer and editor.

THE ANHINGA PRIZE FOR POETRY SERIES

Conversations During Sleep
Michele Wolf, 1997

Man Under a Pear Tree
Keith Ratzlaff, 1996

Easter Vigil
Ann Neelon, 1995

Mass for the Grace of a Happy Death
Frank X. Gaspar, 1994

The Physicist at the Mall
Janet Holmes, 1993

Hat Dancer Blue
Earl S. Braggs, 1992

Hands
Jean Monahan, 1991

*The Long Drive Home**
Nick Bozanic, 1989

Enough Light to See
Julianne Seeman, 1988

*Conversing with the Light**
Will Wells, 1987

*The Whistle Maker**
Robert Levy, 1986

*Perennials**
Judith Kitchen, 1985

The Hawk in the Backyard
Sherry Rind, 1984

Sorting Metaphors
Ricardo Pau-Llosa, 1983

**Out of print*

RECENT BOOKS
FROM ANHINGA PRESS

The Secret History of Water
Silvia Curbelo, 1997

This Once
Nick Bozanic, 1997

*Runaway with Words: A Short Course on Poetry
and How to Take It with You*
Joann Gardner, 1998

*Runaway with Words: A Collection of Poems
from Florida's Youth Shelters*
Edited and Introduced by Joann Gardner, 1997

Walking Back from Woodstock
Earl S. Braggs, 1997

Hello Stranger: Beach Poems
Robert Dana, 1996

*Isle of Flowers:
Poems by Florida's Individual Artist Fellows*
Donna J. Long, Helen Pruitt Wallace, Rick Campbell, eds., 1995

*Unspeakable Strangers:
Descents into the Dark Self, Ascent into the Light*
Van K. Brock, 1995

The Secret Life of Moles
P. V. LeForge, 1992

North of Wakulla: An Anthology
M. J. Ryals and D. Decker, eds., 1988